God Loves You

Written by Carol Rubow

Illustrated by Laura Freeman

CONCORDIA PUBLISHING HOUSE · SAINT LOUIS

Many, many people live in the world.

Some people are tall

and some people are short.

Some people are thin and some people are not.

Some are young people and some are old people.

Many, many people live in the world.

Some of these people love you very much.

Mother loves you. Father loves you.

Grandmother loves you. Grandfather loves you.

Many people love you very much.

Do you know who else loves you very much?

God loves you.

God loves Mother. God loves Father.

God loves Grandmother. God loves Grandfather.

God loves you very much.

Did you know that God made you?

God made everything in the world.

God made the bright, pretty flowers.

God made the tall, tall trees.

God made animals that run. God made animals that hop.
God made birds that fly. God made fish that swim.

God made you.

God made everything in the world.

Did you know that once there was no world?

There were no bright, pretty flowers.

There were no tall, tall trees.

There were no animals that run or hop.

There were no birds that fly.

There were no fish that swim.

There was only God. . . .

God said, "Let there be flowers!"
And there were flowers.

God said, "Let there be trees!"
And there were trees.

God said, "Let there be animals!"
And there were animals.

God made everything in the world.

Can you make a bright, pretty flower?

Can you make a tall, tall tree?

Can you make a real, live rabbit?

No! Nobody can!

There are some things only God can do.

Only God can make the rain fall.

Only God can make the sun shine.

Only God can make the wind blow.

Only God can make the flowers grow.

There is something else only God can do . . .

Only God can see you all the time.

God sees you when you sleep at night.

God sees you when you play outside.

God sees you when you read in school.

God sees you when you pray in church.

God sees you all the time.

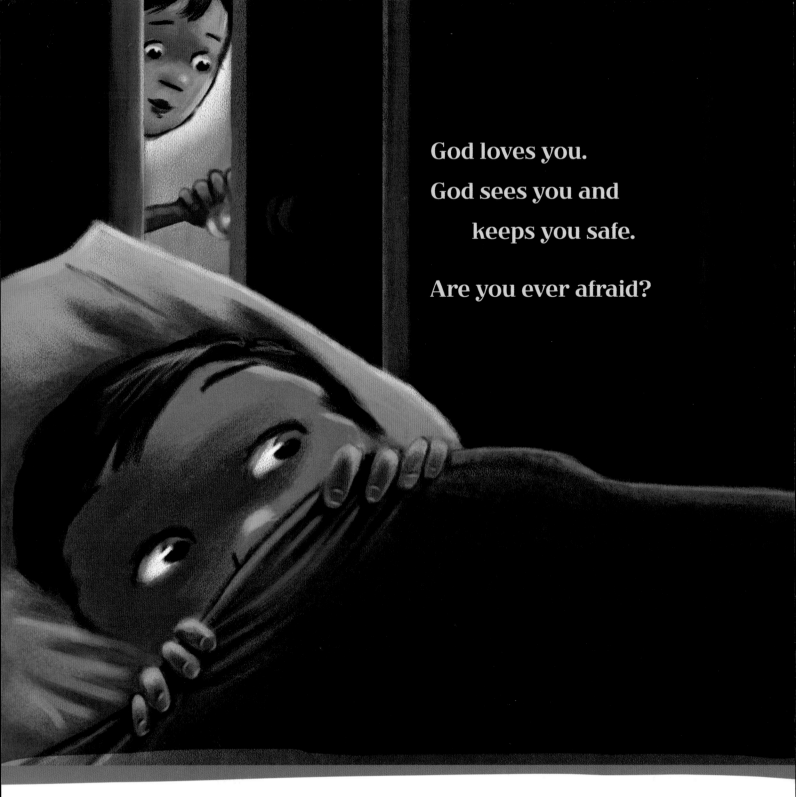

God loves you.
God sees you and
keeps you safe.

Are you ever afraid?

Are you afraid at night when it is very, very dark?
Are you afraid when you hear a loud, loud noise?

God gave you a mother and a father and other people
    to take care of you.
God sends His holy angels to watch over you and keep you safe.

Why does God love people so much?

Why does God give people so many things?

Why does God take care of people?

That is the way God is.

God is love.

God loves all the time!

As God's child, you want to love too.

But do you love all the time?

No?

Sometimes it's hard to love, isn't it?

Sometimes we do things that hurt people.

Sometimes we say things that hurt people.

Sometimes we think things that hurt people.

Your sin makes you do these things.

Sin is doing what you want to do,
not what God wants you to do.

All people are sinners.

But . . . When you feel bad about this, remember:
God still loves you, even when you sin.

God forgives your sin.

God loves you so much . . .

He sent His Son, Jesus, to save all sinners!

Jesus died on the cross for your sin.

Jesus shows how God loves all people.

Jesus shows how God loves you
    even though you sin.

You are God's own dear child.

You can be sure that God forgives your sin.
You can be sure that God loves you.
You can be sure that God
will help you love Him
and all people.

God sends you a special gift to help you love.

God sends His Holy Spirit to live in your heart.
God's Holy Spirit helps you love God.
God's Holy Spirit helps you love other people.
God's Holy Spirit helps you to do the things He wants.

The Holy Spirit is God doing these things in you.

God made you.

God takes care of you.

God forgives your sin because...

God Loves You!